221
MB

RON JON
Custom
SURFBOARDS

RIPCURL

PROTECTION
G-SHOCK

KAROWUI
SURF
CLUB
CALIFORNIA
California
DP 695CT

SUNSET
FCS

THE
JORDAN

SURF CENTER WUSTROW
SURFCENTER WUSTROW
PAINT

35

97549097R00035

Made in the USA
San Bernardino, CA
23 November 2018